Think Like Jesus

Fred Adomako

All scripture quotations, unless otherwise indicated, are taken from the King James Version of the Bible.

Scripture quotations marked NASB are from the New American Standard Bible © 1960, 1962, 1963, 1968, 1971, 1972, 1973, 1975, 1977, 1995 by the Lockman Foundation. Used by permission.

Scripture quotations marked AMP are from the Amplified Bible © 1954, 1958, 1962, 1964, 1965, 1987 by the Lockman Foundation. Used by permission.

Scripture quotations marked NET are from the NET Bible © 1996–2006 by Biblical Studies Press, LLC. All rights reserved.

Think Like Jesus
ISBN 978-0-692-31234-6
Copyright © 2014 by Fred Adomako

Published in the United States by Fred Adomako

Printed in the United States of America. All rights reserved. Contents may not be reproduced without the express written consent of the publisher.

CONTENTS

Introduction v
CHAPTER 1
What Did Jesus Think about Himself? ... 1
CHAPTER 2
The Identity of Jesus 4
CHAPTER 3
The Nature of a Born-Again Christian ... 7
CHAPTER 4
The Purpose of Jesus Christ 13
CHAPTER 5
The Position of Jesus Christ 16
CHAPTER 6
The Personality of Jesus Christ 22
CHAPTER 7
How to Manifest Your Divine Nature ... 24
CHAPTER 8
Oneness with God 38
CHAPTER 9
Healing 42
CHAPTER 10
Wealth and Riches 55
CHAPTER 11
Salvation 71

For as he thinks in his heart, so is he.

(Proverbs 23:7)

Introduction

The life experiences of a person flow out from his heart. Out of the abundance of his heart, he speaks and exhibits life experiences that are consistent with what is going on in his heart. A bad tree cannot yield good fruit. Neither can a good tree yield bad fruit.

The purpose of this book is to reveal the true identity of born-again Christians, help them maintain consciousness about who they are in the spirit, and ultimately rekindle their passion for souls. Before someone becomes born again, his thoughts and actions spring out of his unsaved nature. After he becomes born again, the Christian must now become conscious of his new nature so he can experience a life consistent with his renewed identity.

This book will take you on a journey to reveal the true identity of Jesus Christ and in the process reveal the true identity of born-again Christians. As Jesus is, so are we in this world now! Everything you read about Jesus is also true concerning your born-again spirit at this moment. You are *everything* like Jesus *right now* in your spirit. Have I said that enough? The goal of this book is to present the identity of Jesus

Christ from a perspective that will help you embrace his identity as your new identity and renew your mind accordingly.

Chapter 1

What Did Jesus Think about Himself?

When the Lord Jesus Christ came to the earth in the flesh, he was a unique creature that had never existed before in the history of mankind. His status as a Son of man qualified him as a human being because he was born by another human being, Mary. However, because Jesus was also the Son of God, he was God in his spirit. His flesh was human, but his spirit was divine.

Philippians 2:4 says that "Jesus thought it not robbery to be equal with God although he was in the form of God." Hebrews 1:8–9 also refers to Jesus as God. Jesus did not lose his status as a member of the Trinity when he came to earth. Although he was fully human in his body and soul, he was also fully God in his spirit.

Anyone born of a human takes the nature of a human. Similarly, anyone born of God takes after the spiritual nature of God: "That which is born of the flesh is flesh; and that which is born of the Spirit is spirit" (John 3:6). In the natural, Jesus was the Son of man. However, in the spirit he was the Son of God.

How Humans Identify Themselves

The identity of a person is largely influenced by his parents or other caretakers who raised him. Such parents or caretakers not only name the child but also shape his identity as he grows up. When the child is grown up, he either adopts the identity package he inherited from his parents or caretakers, or he replaces it with a different identity formed from his own life experiences. The identity of a person typically comprises his name, genetics, language, history, nationality, culture, and his parents' or caretakers' experiences.

Throughout his life, a person's thoughts and actions are influenced by his identity. If he embraces his nationality and culture, for example, he will identify with his people—thinking, talking, and basically conducting himself in accordance with his culture. His primary language and the language of his thoughts will be his mother tongue or some other acquired language. Thus a person's identity becomes ingrained in his subconscious mind and heart, constantly influencing him in everything he does throughout his life.

In a nutshell, a person's thoughts and actions are influenced by his identity, and his identity is influenced by his past, present, and future experiences.

The thoughts and actions of a person are influenced by his perception of his own identity.

Chapter 2

The Identity of Jesus

Even as a child, Jesus knew he was the Son of God though born of a human. He understood the importance of coming to earth in the form of a man. Until he started his full-time ministry, he had to submit to his earthly parents while knowing that God was his real Father, and that therefore he was God in a human body (Phil. 2:6). But after he started his ministry, Jesus identified more with his divine heritage than his human heritage. He taught his disciples not to call any man on earth their father, because they had only one Father who is in heaven (Matt. 23:9). There was another instance wherein Jesus told his followers that his mother and brethren are those who do the will of God (Matt. 12:46–50).

By calling God his Father, Jesus was announcing his real identity as God with the same attributes that made God, God (Phil. 2:6 AMP).

I and [my] Father are one. Then the Jews took up stones again to stone him. Jesus answered them, many good works have I shewed you from my Father; for which of those works do ye stone me? The Jews answered him, saying, for a good work we stone thee not; but for blasphemy; and because that thou, being a man, makest thyself God. Jesus answered them, is it not written in your law, I said, Ye are gods? If he called them gods, unto whom the word of God came, and the scripture cannot be broken; say ye of him, whom the Father hath sanctified, and sent into the world, thou blasphemest; because I said, I am the Son of God? (John 10:30–36).

Rather than being consumed by his human nature, Jesus was more conscious of his divine nature, which allowed him to maintain a divine identity instead of a human identity.

Thinking like a mere man produces only natural results. Thinking God's thoughts produces supernatural results.

Chapter 3

The Nature of a Born-Again Christian

When a person becomes born again, he takes on the same nature that Jesus had on earth. The spirit of the born-again Christian is not "born of blood, or of the will of the flesh, or the will of man, but of God" (John 1:13). Therefore, although the born-again Christian has a human body, his status as a son of God qualifies him to be god in his spirit: "Behold, what manner of love the Father hath bestowed upon us, that we should be called the sons of God" (1 John 3:1). When God called us His sons, He made us to partake of His divine nature. As He is, so are we in this world.

Before we became born again, our allegiance was to our earthly cultures and countries. Now that we are born-again, our allegiance to the kingdom of God must supersede any earthly allegiances. Your born-again spirit has a "nationality" that is different from the nationality of your physical body. You must decide how to prioritize your various allegiances. Remember, Jesus had an earthly country as well as a heavenly country. But his affection for heaven far outweighed his affection for Bethlehem.

The issue with our culture and nationality only comes into play when our loyalty to such affiliations holds more value for us than things pertaining to the kingdom of heaven. Philippians 3:20 (NET) says that our citizenship is in heaven. If the Christian continues to identify himself more with his earthly nationality than his heavenly nationality, his thoughts and actions will represent the thoughts and actions of his humanity; they will reflect how things are done in his earthly country. Conversely, if he identifies himself more with his heavenly citizenship than his earthly citizenship, then his thoughts and actions will represent the thoughts and actions of his divinity; in this case, they will begin to reflect how things are done in heaven.

> The first man is of the earth, earthy: the second man is the Lord from heaven. As is the earthy, such are they also that

are earthy: and as is the heavenly, such are they also that are heavenly. And as we have borne the image of the earthy, we shall [and so let us [AMP]] also bear the image of the heavenly (1 Cor. 15:47–49).…

Wherefore henceforth know we no man after the flesh: yea, though we have known Christ after the flesh, yet now henceforth know we him no more. Therefore, if any man be in Christ, he is a new creature: old things are passed away; behold, all things are become new (2 Cor. 5:16–17).

The born-again Christian is no longer a "mere man" (1 Cor. 3:4 NASB) subject to human limitations. But if he continues to identify himself solely with his humanity, he will continue to think and behave as a mere man. On the other hand, if he renews the spirit of his mind with the word of God and accepts his new identity as a son of God, which makes him one with God, then his thoughts and actions will be like God's.

In his divinity, the Christian regains the dominion that Adam lost in the garden. Jesus demonstrated his dominion when he exercised complete control over everything he encountered. One of the purposes of salvation is to restore man from limited human experiences to unlimited divine experiences—from a bound humanity to a free divinity. God's plan is for His children, in their divinity, to have complete power and authority over everything in this world (Heb. 2:6–10).

As the heavens are higher than the earth, so are the thoughts and ways of your divine nature higher than the thoughts and ways of your human nature.

If you believe that you are just human, you will think and act like a human only; your thoughts and actions will be based on your human identity, circumstances, and limitations. However, if you believe that you are one with God through Jesus Christ, then you will think and act just like God thinks and acts. Your thoughts, in this case, will be based on God's identity, power, and unlimited resources.

The obvious step now is to shed more light on our divine nature. What does it mean to partake of God's divine nature? After we discuss that question, we will then discuss what the Bible says about how we can operate in our divinity.

The way to know more about our divine nature is to know more about Jesus' divine nature. So let's go into scripture and see what more we can find about Jesus' identity.

__Chapter 4__

The Purpose of Jesus Christ

The divine nature of Jesus can be examined by taking a closer look at his purpose. Many scriptures highlight the fact that Jesus' only purpose was to do his Father's will. He was not consumed with his own agenda or personal goals. Jesus' food and drink was to do the will of his Father and to finish the work his Father sent him to do (John 4:34; Heb. 10:7).

Jesus knew that he was not an independent God, because there is, in fact, only one God and Jesus Christ is His offspring or extension. Think about Jesus' analogy about the vine and the branches. His identity as God is based on his Father's identity as God. Without his Father, he would have operated as a regular human bound by human limitations.

God allowed Jesus to exhibit complete supremacy over every aspect of humanity because Jesus was advancing *only* the will of his Father. From a very early age, Jesus' mind-set was centered on doing his Father's will and pleasing him. He submitted his will to his Father's will although he had the same qualities that made God, God (Phil. 2:6 AMP). Not even a shameful and painful death on a tree could prevent Jesus from pursuing his Father's will.

As we can see, one of the major characteristics of Jesus' divine nature is his divine purpose of fulfilling his Father's will to save man.

The divine purpose of the Christian is the same purpose that Jesus has; which is to save man. While the role of Jesus in God's plan for salvation was to shed his blood for the remission of sin, the Christian's role is to tell the story about the gospel of Jesus Christ with the hope of leading people to salvation.

While God wants His children to succeed in their human purpose, He wants them to also prioritize their divine purpose over their human purpose: "Seek ye first the kingdom of God and His righteousness and all these things shall be added unto you" (Matt. 6:33). Therefore, the Christian should use his personal goals or purpose to help achieve his divine purpose: "He who says that he is living in him, will do as he did" (1 John 2:6).

You can exercise your divine authority and power only when your will is submitted to God's will. In your divinity, you get to reign over everything in life, just like Jesus did.

Chapter 5

The Position of Jesus Christ

The divinity of Jesus Christ can also be explained by his position as a member of the holy Trinity. As God the Son, Jesus' position is at the right hand of God the Father in heaven, from where he reigns as Lord over everything forever.

We cannot discuss the position of Jesus Christ without discussing his power. Jesus Christ declared after his resurrection that he had been given all the power in heaven and on earth. In fact, God has commanded all His angels to worship Jesus Christ and has given him a name above every other name. Therefore, Jesus Christ has power over everything and everyone in heaven (except God the Father), in this world and in the world to come. He is Lord over everything! Moreover, all things were created by him—things in heaven and on earth, both visible and invisible, including thrones, dominions, principalities, and powers. All of them were created by him and for him.

Through his blood, Jesus Christ paved the way for his believers to share in his position as part of the Godhead. God has made believers heirs of God and joint-heirs with Christ Jesus, and has allowed them to sit together in heavenly places in Christ Jesus (Eph. 2:6). When someone becomes born again, his spirit unites with the spirit of Jesus Christ and becomes one spirit. God gives the believer His Holy Spirit as a gift! Jesus said, "I am in my Father, and ye in me, and I in you" (John 14:20). There is no difference between the spirit of a born-again Christian and the spirit of Jesus Christ. There is only one Spirit (Eph. 4:3–4) expressing Himself in different roles through different born-again believers.

As a result of our union with Christ, God has raised us up to share in the same position as Jesus Christ, although we completely submit ourselves to Christ as the head of the body.

Furthermore, if believers have inherited the same spirit that was in Jesus Christ, then we can conclude that we have also inherited the past, present, and future experiences of that same Spirit. That means that *all* of Jesus Christ's actions can be credited to his believers who have united with him. Those actions include creating the universe, obeying God, performing all those miracles, being crucified, being resurrected, and being exalted to the right hand of God.

In Hebrews 7:9–10, the Bible explains a principle that when Abraham paid his tithes, Levi, who was not even born at the time, also paid tithes because he was in the loins of Abraham. That principle also explains how Adam's sin affected everyone. Since we were all in Adam's loins when he disobeyed God, we participated in Adam's disobedience: "For as by one man's disobedience many were made sinners, so by the obedience of one shall many be made righteous" (Rom. 5:17). If Adam had not disobeyed God, we would have inherited the exact image and likeness of God from Adam. Instead, we were born in the image and likeness of a sinful man stripped of his divine nature.

The sin that Adam and Eve committed separated them from their godlike nature. Prior to their disobedience, their human nature was overshadowed by that divine nature that caused them to live like God on the earth. After their disobedience, the curse they received that day was only an explanation of what they (and all their descendants) were to expect as mere powerless humans without their divine nature.

The same way we shared in Adam's sinful human nature, we now share in Jesus' righteous divine nature after we are born again. In Romans 11:16–17, the Bible says this: "For if the firstfruit [is] holy, the lump [is] also [holy]; and if the root [is] holy, so [are] the branches. And if some of the branches were broken off, and you, being a wild olive tree, were grafted in among them, and with them became a partaker of the root and fatness of the olive tree, do not boast against the branches."

That scripture also explains how the status of Jesus Christ is conferred upon believers when they become one with him. When we become born again, we disconnect from our Adamic roots and connect to our new roots in Christ Jesus. Just as Adam's actions were credited to us due to our union with him, Jesus' actions are credited to us when we become one with him. When God grafted us in Christ, He allowed us to share not only in the nature of Jesus Christ but also in his past, present, and future actions.

So now we are righteous because Jesus is righteous, we were dead because he was dead, we are risen because he is risen, we are seated in heavenly places because he is seated in heavenly places, we are healed because he is healed, we are rich because he is rich, we live forever because he lives forever, and we have all power and authority because Jesus has all power and authority. As he is, so are we in this world!

The divine nature of Jesus Christ is also demonstrated through his position.

For thus saith the high and lofty One that inhabiteth eternity, whose name is Holy; I dwell in the high and holy place, with him also that is of a contrite and humble spirit, to revive the spirit of the humble, and revive the heart of the contrite ones.

(Isaiah 57:17)

Chapter 6

The Personality of Jesus Christ

If we could sum up the nature of Jesus Christ in one word, that word would be *love*! Jesus is the exact image of God expressed in human form. He is full of grace, truth, faith, compassion, and mercy, just like his Father. A key feature of Jesus' personality is his humility. He is meek and lowly in heart. His position as the Son of the Almighty God did not prevent him from going on his knees and washing the dirty feet of his disciples.

His kindness and compassion allowed him to give up everything, including his own life, to save the life of another.

His grace and mercy prompts him to forgive anyone who hurts him. While they crucified him, he responded by saying, "Father, forgive them, for they know not what they do."

With his power, he advocates for the weak and delivers them from all kinds of oppression.

He is always truthful and seeking the welfare of others.

That is the divine nature that we have inherited. We are the exact image of Jesus Christ in our spirit. His personality will manifest in our lives if we think like him and accept his personality as our personality.

Chapter 7

How to Manifest Your Divine Nature

There are several levels of glory when it comes to manifesting the divine nature of God in you. In 2 Corinthians 3:18, this glory is described as an ever-increasing splendor, the pinnacle of which is the very image of Jesus Christ. Jesus Christ is the ultimate glory of God because he was the manifested word of God in the flesh. From the moment a person hears the word of God, the will of God is for him to become progressively acquainted with the word until that word becomes alive in him. It is put this way in 2 Peter 1:19: "We have also a more sure word of prophesy; whereunto ye do well that ye take heed, as unto a light that shineth in a dark place, until the day dawn, and the day star arise [comes into being – [AMP version]] in your hearts." By getting more revelation about any word of God, believers progress from one level of glory to higher levels of glory, until the point where they become one with that word in their physical bodies. You see, the word of God is a living

Spirit, and for that matter, invisible. So in order for the invisible word of God to be manifested in a physical world, the word needs to be wrapped in a physical body so that it can be seen, felt, heard, smelled, and otherwise experienced. God manifested His Word to us when His Word took on a physical body in the person of Jesus Christ.

For more clarity, let's use the following example: When you read about any subject in the Bible (let's say, Peace), the will of God is that you not only *know* about peace and *act* peacefully, but also become one with Peace in your heart and mind. In that oneness, your mind becomes consumed with the nature of Peace while your body yields to the promptings of Peace and begins to manifest peaceful actions. Peace is a spirit of God that must have a physical body to manifest himself in a physical world.

Jesus Christ in the flesh was the embodiment of every word of God in one physical body! So, for example, when Jesus said, "Peace, be still," he was not speaking from mere knowledge about the peace of God. Rather, it was Peace himself doing what he does by calming a chaotic situation. That's the nature of Peace. Similarly, when you turn on any light, the nature of that light is to brighten a dark area. The same principle applies to every word of God. Love loves, Joy brings joy, Righteousness acts righteous, Grace is gracious, etc.

Therefore, the level of manifestation (glory) of the word of God you are experiencing is directly related to how much of your mind has been renewed to sync with the mind of Jesus Christ.

The ultimate glory of the word of God is its embodiment in the physical body of a person.

You cannot change the fruit of a tree unless you change its roots. Before we were saved, we were rooted in Adam, who was a living soul and one devoid of eternal life. As a result, the fruit that we bore originated from our sinful Adamic nature.

Adam could manifest the word of God in the physical world only when his spirit was connected to the Spirit of God. In that condition, his mind was in sync with the mind of God. When it came to naming the living creatures, Adam gave them the exact names that God had in mind. For example, when Adam called his wife's name

"Woman" he did not invent the name out of thin air. Rather, a few verses up, the Bible said God made a "woman." So before God brought her to Adam to see what Adam would call her, God already knew that what He had created was in fact a "woman." I believe the name-calling job God gave Adam was His way of assessing how connected Adam's mind was to His mind. Adam was able to pick up what God was thinking in his own mind because of his spiritual connection to God. Every name he called each animal, "that *was* its name" (Gen. 2:19). In other words, those names were exactly the names God had in mind for those animals. Remember, God created the animals before He created Adam. And He knew exactly what He was creating before He created every single one of those animals.

Since Adam was not a life-giving spirit, he needed his connection to the Spirit of God in order to manifest the word of God in the physical world. When he lost his spiritual connection to God, Adam lost the ability to manifest any word of God in the physical world, since he was not a life-giving spirit and therefore spiritually dead.

Although God offered Adam the free gift of eternal life by giving him free access to the tree of life, Adam chose the serpent's alternative of death by eating from the tree of the knowledge of good and evil.

On the contrary, Jesus Christ is a life-giving spirit: "*The first man, Adam, became a living soul.* The last Adam *became* a life-giving spirit" (1 Cor. 15:45 NASB); "For as the Father hath life in himself, so hath he given to the Son to have life in himself" (John 5:26). Unlike Adam, Jesus is a life source himself. Jesus is able to give life to any dead situation in the physical world. That is the main difference between our old Adamic nature and our new Christlike nature. Instead of being just a living soul, the believer is now a life-giving spirit that lives in a physical body: "He that hath the Son hath life" (1 John 5:12). The mental transition toward accepting our new Christlike nature is the key to manifesting our divinity. That brings us to the next point about the example Jesus gave the disciples on that subject.

Let's take a trip to the holy mountain of transfiguration and discuss in detail Jesus' example about how he revealed his glory to Peter, James, and John in Mark 9:2–9.

> And after six days Jesus taketh Peter, James, and John his brother, and bringeth them up into an high mountain apart, and was transfigured before them: and his face did shine as the sun, and his raiment was white as the light. And, behold, there appeared unto them Moses and Elias talking with him. Then answered Peter, and said unto Jesus, Lord, it is good for us to be here: if thou wilt, let us make here three tabernacles; one for thee, and one for Moses, and one for Elias. While he yet spake, behold, a bright cloud overshadowed them: and behold a voice out of the cloud, which said, This is my beloved Son, in whom I am well pleased; hear ye him. And when the disciples heard [it], they fell on their face, and were sore afraid. And Jesus came and touched them, and said, Arise, and be not afraid. And when they had lifted up their eyes, they saw no man, save Jesus only. And as they came down from the mountain, Jesus charged them, saying,

Tell the vision to no man, until the Son of man be risen again from the dead.

The word "transfigured" is translated from the Greek word "metamorphoo," which means to change into another form. Jesus transformed himself from his human form to his divine form right before the disciples' eyes. The word "metamorphoo" is used four times in the Bible, and the first two appearances of that word are found in the transfiguration story in the gospels of Matthew and Mark. The next two uses of the word are found in the following verses: *"But we all, with open face beholding as in a glass the glory of the Lord, are changed* [metamorphoo] *into the same image from glory to glory, [even] as by the Spirit of the Lord" (2 Cor. 3:18).*

In this instance, the Bible is saying that the level of manifestation of the word of God (Jesus Christ) in our lives is directly related to the level of revelation we have about Jesus Christ. In 1 John 3:2, the Bible says that "when he [Jesus Christ] shall appear [manifest], we shall be like him; for we shall see him as he is." That scripture is referring not only to the second coming of

Christ, but also to the countless times you get a new revelation about Jesus Christ. Each scripture is loaded with various degrees of revelation. Therefore, your divine nature will manifest according to your level of revelation of Jesus Christ (the word of God). For example, the more revelation you get about the mercy of Jesus Christ, the more you can manifest mercy in this physical world. Don't forget that you are already like Jesus in your spirit. Our goal here is to bring out who you are in your spirit so that it can be experienced with the five senses.

> The word "metamorphoo" is also used in Romans 12:2 as follows: "And be not conformed to this world: but be ye transformed [metamorphoo] by the renewing of your mind, that ye may prove what [is] that good, and acceptable, and perfect, will of God."

Clearly, Romans 12:2 is showing us that we can transform (metamorphoo) into our divine nature by renewing our minds: "As a man thinketh in his heart, so is he." So who do you say that you are? When you think about yourself, what comes to your mind? When anyone is in Christ, he loses his old nature. He is no longer the same human being *acting* like a son of God—no. Rather, he *becomes* a son of God and therefore part of the holy Trinity—Father, Son, and the Holy Ghost. By becoming one with Jesus Christ, we get to partake of his position in the holy Trinity and join the Godhead as sons of God. Our bodies become the physical manifestation of the unseen God: "For we are members of his body, of his flesh, and of his bones" (Eph. 5:30). Because of Jesus Christ, we are no longer separated from God. We have united with God the Father, God the Son, and God the Holy Ghost into *one* God. If Jesus is one with God, and we are one with Jesus, then we are one with God: "For in Him the whole fullness of Deity (the Godhead) continues to dwell in bodily form [giving complete expression of the divine nature]. And you are in Him, made full and having come to fullness of life [in Christ you too are filled with the Godhead—Father, Son and Holy Spirit—and reach full spiritual stature]" (Col. 2:9 AMP).

Therefore, Romans 12:2 is asking us to renew our minds to think like God thinks so that we can manifest God's divine nature in our physical bodies, which become available as a living sacrifice in the process.

The degree of God's manifestation in our lives is directly related to the degree our minds are conformed to His mind in any situation and on any issue. The word of God is the mind of God.

If we think and set our minds according to our old human nature (our living-soul nature), we experience death—that is, powerlessness resulting from separation from God. However, if we think and set our minds according to the Spirit (our life-giving Spirit), we experience life—that is, reconnection to God's power through Jesus Christ: "For they that are after the flesh do mind the things of the flesh; but they that are after the Spirit the things of the Spirit. For to be carnally minded [is] death; but to be spiritually minded [is] life and peace" (Rom. 8:5–6). The word of God is the Spirit of God. Jesus said, "The words that I speak unto you, [they] are spirit, and [they] are life" (John 6:63). Therefore, if we think and set our minds according to the word of God, we experience life. Like a light switch, the believer can turn on the power of God in his life when his mind becomes one with the mind of Christ.

The body of man is influenced by his soul (mind, feelings, and emotions) as well as his spirit. The soul of man has a choice in determining whether his spirit will be reconnected to the Spirit of God. When a person becomes born again, his spirit is reunited with the Spirit of God. He becomes a new creature, a God Spirit in a human body. His body will be influenced by his new Spirit when his mind is set according to the word of God. If he fails to set his mind according to his new Spirit, his body will continue to reflect the nature and promptings of his old unsaved spirit. For example, Adam and "woman" experienced death in the garden when they set their minds according to the word of the devil and allowed the devil to express itself through their physical bodies.

When we set our minds according to the Spirit, Jesus Christ expresses himself through our physical bodies: "I am crucified with Christ: nevertheless I live; yet not I, but Christ liveth in me: and the life which I now live in the flesh I live by the faith of the Son of God, who loved me, and gave himself for me" (Gal. 2:20).

So what is the mind of the Spirit? Our example is Jesus. Let's move on to more specific topics and discuss the mind-set of Jesus on them.

Chapter 8

Oneness with God

Let this mind be in you, which was also in Christ Jesus: Who, being in the form of God, thought it not robbery to be equal with God: But made himself of no reputation, and took upon him the form of a servant, and was made in the likeness of men: And being found in fashion as a man, he humbled himself, and became obedient unto death, even the death of the cross. Wherefore God also hath highly exalted him, and given him a name which is above every name: That at the name of Jesus every knee should bow, of [things] in heaven, and [things] in earth, and [things] under the earth; And [that] every tongue should confess that Jesus Christ [is] Lord, to the glory of God the Father.

(Philippians 2:5–11)

In the mind of Jesus, he knew that he was just like his Father in every way. Whatever makes God, God, can be found in Jesus as well. Nevertheless, because of his love for his Father, Jesus decided he would do anything, including suffering a painful death, to please Him. And suffer he did! Isaiah says Jesus was despised and rejected of men; a man of sorrows and acquainted with grief. In the gospels, the Bible recorded the King of Glory washing the feet of his servants and being betrayed, spat at, slapped around, stripped naked and scorned in public, lashed till his skin was raw, and nailed to a tree before finally dying a shameful and excruciating death!

The humility of Jesus Christ is exemplified by the fact that while he knew he had the power to stop all the suffering with one word, he never once opened his mouth in his defense! He reasoned that how would the scripture be fulfilled if he used his power to stop the suffering? "He was oppressed, and he was afflicted, yet he opened not his mouth: he is brought as a lamb to the slaughter, and as a sheep before her shearers is dumb, so he openeth not his mouth" (Isa. 53:7). As a result, God resurrected Jesus from the dead and exalted him high above all else.

Jesus' example shows us that although we should always be conscious of our new divine nature, we are to mentally put on the "towel of a servant" (as in John 13:4) and seek the will of God in every situation, rather than advance our own contrary desires.

Through our oneness with Christ, we can also think it not robbery to be equal with God, because we have the same Spirit of God in us. As God is, so are we in this world. Although we have a human body and soul, our spirit is the Spirit of God himself. Therefore, the essence of who we are is God in a human body. And just like Jesus, we are completely submitted to the Father's will in every situation.

Chapter 9

Healing

So what did Jesus think about healing? When we set our minds according to the mind of Christ, our physical bodies will also experience the life of God in the area of healing. In his mind, Jesus knew that he had the power and authority to heal all manner of sickness and disease. As a result, he used that power to set people free from the captivity of sickness and disease.

Here is the mind of Christ on healing: "The Spirit of the Lord [is] upon me, because he hath anointed me to preach the gospel to the poor; he hath sent me to heal the brokenhearted, to preach deliverance to the captives, and recovering of sight to the blind, to set at liberty them that are bruised, to preach the acceptable year of the Lord" (Luke 4:18). Jesus' mind stayed on the truth that he was the healer, the one sent by God to heal the sick.

From the beginning, God did not create man with any type of sickness. In fact, when He finished creating the world, God said everything He had created was "very good." Adam was therefore experiencing only good things until he decided to taste fruit from the tree of the knowledge of good and evil. From that moment on, he became acquainted with all kinds of evil things leading to death. As a result of Adam's transgression, it became human nature to cave in to sickness and to take possession of it whenever it hit the body. For example, someone who accepts the presence of pain in his head might take possession of that pain by thinking or saying something like, "I *have* a headache."

However, because of the stripes he received on his back, Jesus paid the price for his believers to have his thoughts that they have the power to reject sickness in their own bodies, as well as the anointing to heal others. His obedience qualified us to receive the Spirit of God to help us maintain the same thoughts he had on healing: "The Spirit of the Lord [is] upon me, because he hath anointed me to preach the gospel to the poor; he hath sent me to heal the brokenhearted, to preach deliverance to the captives, and recovering of sight to the blind, to set at liberty them that are bruised, to preach the acceptable year of the Lord."

When our minds are overwhelmed with the word of God, our bodies will be overwhelmed with the power of God. Every mind-set of sickness, disease, or any kind of physical impairment or infirmity must be replaced with the mind-set of Christ on healing. By thinking the thoughts of Jesus, rather than the thoughts of sickness, the believer ignites the power of God for healing and allows his body to come under the power of the word of God while he disconnects from the power of sickness and disease.

Simply maintaining a mind-set that the Spirit of the Lord is upon you is very significant. Jesus told the disciples that they would receive power after that the Holy Ghost has come upon them! After the Holy Spirit came upon them, they were able to do amazing things beyond their own natural abilities. The Spirit of the Lord upon Mary caused her to have a baby without a man! The Spirit of the Lord upon the face of the waters caused the waters and the earth to come alive and bring forth fishes, birds, animals, and trees! The Spirit of the Lord upon a piece of dust and ashes caused it to start breathing and speaking! The Spirit of the Lord upon Jesus anointed him to rule over everything in life! By maintaining the mind-set that the Spirit of the Lord is upon you, you will yield yourself completely to the directions and power of the Holy Spirit. If you have received the baptism of the Holy Spirit, then you already have the Spirit of the Lord in you and upon you. Therefore, you need only to set your mind on the thoughts of the Holy Spirit to allow him free reign over your body. The thoughts of the Holy Spirit are the thoughts of Jesus Christ.

The key here is to *maintain* the thoughts of Christ in our minds: "Thou wilt keep him in perfect peace, whose mind is stayed on thee: because he trusteth in thee" (Isa. 26:3). As a spirit-filled believer, you will never be disconnected from the power of God. However, your mind-set is the switch that turns on the power of God in your life. It takes faith in God to allow your mind to remain rested on His word when the pain and discomfort of sickness are screaming for attention in your mind.

If you believe that by becoming one with Christ, all of his actions have been credited to you, then you must believe also that your victory over all manner of sicknesses and diseases actually took place more than two thousand years ago, when Jesus healed all manner of sicknesses and diseases! "For as by one man's disobedience many were made sinners, so also by one Man's obedience many will be made righteous" (Rom. 5:19). If it was valid for Adam's sin to be credited to us, then it is equally valid for the works of Jesus Christ to be credited to us! That means that when Jesus performed all those miracles, you also performed all those miracles, because you are one with him! When Jesus was crucified, you were crucified with him! When he rose up, you rose up with him! Every single action of Jesus Christ has been credited to us as a result of our oneness with him!

Understand that Jesus did not only die for us but also lived (and continues to live) for us, that his life may serve as a foundation upon which we can spring into the future fully assured of all the benefits of his victories.

What you need to do is believe and accept the works of Jesus Christ as your works and enter into his rest as the reigning and everlasting champion over the enemy. When you enter into his rest, you will cease from your own works and attempts to defeat the enemy over and over again. The battle is over! The works of Jesus Christ are *enough*! You don't need to give the enemy any rematch. When the enemy attacks you, he presents you with false evidence that is designed to make you think contrary to the thoughts of Christ. So remember to pull down those wrong thoughts and replace them with the thoughts of Jesus Christ. Focus on the finished works of Christ, because that is how *you* overcame that sickness more than two thousand years ago.

The miracle for your healing has already taken place! So align your thoughts with the thoughts of Jesus, and accept his victory over sickness and disease as your victory.

Our precious Jesus did it *all* for us!

So now you have a history of healing the sick, casting out devils, feeding thousands of people with only five loaves and two fishes, dying on the cross, rising from the dead, and being seated in heavenly places in Christ Jesus, all because of what Jesus did.

It is hard for the finite mind to grasp the foregoing concept, especially considering that we were not even physically born at the time. However, that is not how God thinks. Although we were not physically present when Adam was eating from the forbidden tree, God found us equally guilty since we were one with Adam. Likewise, although we were not physically present when Jesus was doing all those works, by becoming one with Christ, God has credited all of Jesus' actions to us.

The main reason we can confidently receive all the works of Jesus as our works is that the same Spirit that was in Jesus Christ has united with our spirit into one Spirit. Therefore, when we received the Holy Spirit, his history became our history. The Bible has mentioned that he that is joined with Christ is one spirit. Through the born-again process, God nailed our sinful works to the cross and replaced them with the perfect works of Jesus by allowing us to inherit the same spirit that was in Jesus Christ. So now we are saved not by our own works of righteousness, but by the works of righteousness that Jesus performed. His works included every single thing he did to obey God, such as healing the sick, raising the dead, dying on the cross, rising up again, etc. By dying on the cross, Jesus was able to release his perfect spirit into anyone who believed in him so that they could also share in his perfect works. That is how God justifies us when we believe in Jesus Christ: by replacing our past with the past of Jesus Christ.

Not only that, but the life that we inherited from Jesus was not simply the breath of life or the ability to live forever in heaven—rather, the life of Jesus encompasses the absolute fullness of his experiences and actions, past, present, and future! In other words, the eternal life we received from Jesus is a life that has no beginning or end, and one that is full of only good works!

Therefore, Jesus gave us his life so that we may share in all the benefits that go along with his life. If we don't receive *all* of his past as our past, we will limit ourselves from reaping the full benefits of all that he has accomplished.

With the Bible serving as the recorded history, present, and future of Jesus, we are able to locate ourselves in him even before the foundations of the world and claim all of his actions as our actions! And God completely agrees, because He is the one who loved us so dearly that He gave us such everlasting life!

Since you have already defeated sickness and disease, remind yourself of that and hold the thoughts of Jesus in your mind: "The Spirit of the Lord [is] upon me, because he hath anointed me to preach the gospel to the poor; he hath sent me to heal the brokenhearted, to preach deliverance to the captives, and recovering of sight to the blind, to set at liberty them that are bruised, to preach the acceptable year of the Lord."

The enemy knows that when you keep your mind on the things of the Spirit (the mind of Christ), it is only a matter of time before you see the physical manifestation of what you have been thinking about. As a result, his goal is to either steal the word or distract you from focusing on the word of God. After Jesus explained the parable of the sower he said, "Take heed what ye hear. With the same measure you use, it will be measured to you; and to you who hear, more will be given" (Mark 4:24).

Your manifestation also depends on how much attention you give to the thoughts of Christ. God promises to keep us in perfect peace (which is also translated as soundness in health) when we keep our minds stayed on His word. In 2 Peter 1:19, it says, "And so we have the prophetic word confirmed, which you do well to HEED as a light that shines in a dark place, until the day dawns and the morning star rises in your hearts." In other words, when you remind yourself of God's word, you should allow the word to be consummated in your heart as well. Jesus said in John 14:21 that "he that loveth me [the word of God] shall be loved of my Father, and I will love him, and will manifest myself to him."

As believers, we do not abort the thoughts of Christ and focus on what the sickness wants us to believe. Rather, we carry the thoughts of Christ in our minds until those thoughts penetrate our hearts and become rooted in our souls. And then out of our hearts will flow rivers of living water directing our bodies into perfect healing.

It is important to note here that one must first believe in the finished works of Jesus before he can see the manifestation of those works in the natural. By the stripes of Jesus, you are already healed. What we are discussing here is how to manifest, in the natural, what has already been accomplished by Jesus Christ.

Chapter 10

Wealth and Riches

Here is the mind-set of Jesus on wealth and riches: "All things that the Father hath are mine" (John 16:15). Jesus also said this: "And all mine are thine, and thine are mine" (John 17:10). According to John 13, Jesus knew that the Father had given him *all* things. All things include the earth and its fullness, the seas and their fullness, the heavens and all the hosts of them, the world and all that dwell in it, the visible and invisible worlds, thrones, principalities, dominions, powers, and the world to come. God gave *everything* to Jesus because Jesus and his Father are one, and all that belongs to the Father also belongs to Jesus. John 1 says that Jesus came into the world that was made by him; there was nothing made that was made without him: "All things were created by him and for him" (Col. 1:16).

Before Adam fell, he had free access to and control over everything God made. He had in abundance everything he needed to enjoy life. However, his disobedience separated him from God's provisions and introduced him to a world of lack and insufficiency. Since then, every one of Adam's descendants has been acquainted with limited resources in an economic system that is based on scarcity. People now have to satisfy their needs by exchanging what they have for what they don't have.

Adam's mind-set changed from abundance to lack after he brought the curse upon himself. He had to change his mind. He was kicked out of a place where he had an abundance of everything, to a dry land where he now had to toil and sweat before he could even get food to eat. All of his thoughts became influenced by his lack. For example, before they disobeyed God, Adam and his wife never once thought about the need for clothes, because the glory of God covered their nakedness. But when their disobedience disconnected them from God's supply, their thoughts became influenced by their lack of clothes, which moved them into actions to cover their nakedness. That became the story of Adam and his descendants. In an effort to meet his needs, Adam had to rely on his own limited abilities rather than depend on God's unlimited abilities. Until a person becomes born again and renews his mind, every single one of his thoughts and actions, no matter how intelligent, will be influenced by some type of personal lack. That basic mind-set of lack is the cursed mind-set that controlled Adam's thoughts and actions after he was separated from God. Rich or poor, man's mind-set of scarcity continues until he becomes born again and switches from the Adamic mind-set of scarcity to Christ's mind-set of abundance. In Adam, we were cursed; in Christ, we are blessed.

As you can see, there is a sharp difference between the mind-set of Jesus and the mind-set we inherited from Adam. In the Adamic mind-set, because we lack something, we are always thinking about how to get. However, in the mind-set of Christ, because we have an abundance of all things, we are always thinking about how to give.

The first step in manifesting the wealth and riches of God is to renew your mind to conform to the mind of Christ on wealth and riches: "All things that the Father hath are mine…And all mine are thine, and thine are mine."

As we just saw, the Adamic mind-set of scarcity will always prompt us to accumulate as many resources for ourselves as possible, while Christ's mind-set of abundance will always prompt us to give as many resources as possible to support the weak. Jesus said, "It is more blessed to give than to receive" (Acts 20:35) because giving is associated with the abundance of the giver, while receiving is associated with the receiver's lack.

Understand that what makes a person rich and wealthy is not necessarily the abundance of his possessions. Rather, a person is rich and wealthy because of his reconnection to God. Unless that person is reconciled with God, he is still poor, wretched, miserable, blind, and naked, just like Adam after his fall (Rev. 3:17). True riches come from Jesus Christ. If you have Christ, you have an abundance of all things, including abundance of material wealth and possessions, abundant life, abundant love, abundant joy, abundant peace, abundant health, abundant favor, abundant faith, abundant virtue, abundant power, abundant authority, abundant wholeness, abundant kindness, abundant goodness, abundant self-control, abundant righteousness, abundant grace, abundance of God's word, and abundance of God Himself in you!

Manifesting your wealth and riches as a believer is a function of your mind-set. After becoming born again, the believer must be renewed in the spirit of his mind to conform to the mind of Christ. If deep down in his heart, the believer continues to see himself as just human, then his human limitations will cause him to think like a mere man, and thinking like a mere man is thinking after the flesh, while thinking after the flesh results in actions and outcomes not influenced by the life and power of God. In fact, those types of thoughts are opposite to God's way of thinking. Thoughts of poverty, lack, and insufficiency are dead thoughts because they are enmity against God.

On the other hand, if the believer accepts that he is now a member of the Godhead through Jesus Christ, then he will begin to think like God. His thoughts will now be influenced by the unlimited riches of God in Christ Jesus. In this case, he will think rich and wealthy thoughts, such as, "All things that the Father hath are mine, and all mine are God's." That is how to take possession of your wealth and riches—by believing and maintaining a mind-set that all that the Father has *is already* yours!

As a believer, you already know that you do not need to wait for physical evidence to believe that you are rich and wealthy. If God's word says that you are rich and wealthy, then you are rich and wealthy, regardless of your circumstances. In fact, the source of all wealth and riches abides in you! All the gold, silver, diamonds, oil, and land, and every good thing of monetary value in this world, came out of the word of God! And if the word of God abides in you, then you have the power of all wealth and riches abiding in you.

Throughout the Bible, we see various examples, from the prophets to Jesus, of how the power of God for wealth and riches was manifested to the glory of God. In one instance, we saw Elijah multiplying the barrel of meal and the cruise of oil for a widow. In another instance, Elisha turned a widow's small pot of oil into many vessels of oil, enough to help the poor widow pay off her bills and live on the rest! Solomon used that power to become the richest man in the world during his time! Jesus demonstrated that power when he asked Peter to cast his nets for a boat-sinking catch! We can spend the rest of this book discussing several ways men of God displayed God's power over lack and insufficiency. All you have to understand at this point is that that same power abides in you richly, and the way to ignite that power is by first conforming your mind to the mind of Jesus.

In the preceding chapters, we saw that Jesus gave us a completed life full of victories over everything in this world and the world to come. By virtue of our oneness with him, his fully led life has become our *own* past, present, and future. That also means that when Jesus overcame poverty, lack, and insufficiency, we also overcame poverty, lack, and insufficiency with him.

Now the spoils of Jesus' victory over poverty, lack, and insufficiency have been left for the benefit of believers as they advance the kingdom of God. Everything Jesus needed to fulfill his assignment was made readily available to him. Likewise, everything we need to advance the kingdom of God is waiting for us. As you already know, the wealth and riches we inherited from Jesus are not in some earthly bank account with Jesus' name on it. Rather, Jesus has laid up wealth and riches in heaven for his believers to enjoy not only in heaven, but also on earth.

    With our minds set on Jesus' thoughts, wisdom is transmitted to us about what to do in any given situation. The Spirit of God will inspire us with witty inventions, concepts, and ideas to manifest our authority over lack. Proverbs 4:7 reminds us that "wisdom is the principal thing. Therefore get wisdom, and in all your getting, get understanding." Also, 1 Corinthians tells us that Christ is the wisdom and power of God. Therefore, along with Christ, God gave us wisdom and power to reign over lack and insufficiency. By aligning our thoughts with the thoughts of Christ, all the treasures of wisdom that are hidden in Christ flow freely into our minds. That wisdom is what will direct our decisions and actions in response to lack and insufficiency in ways that manifest our abundant wealth and riches in glory by Christ Jesus.

Speaking of wisdom, Proverbs 3:16 (NET) says that "long life is in her left hand; in her right hand are riches and honor."

Without maintaining the mind-set of Christ on wealth and riches, all our responses to lack and insufficiency would only correspond to our human limitations. Jesus illustrated this concept when he told the disciples to feed five thousand hungry men in the middle of nowhere. They asked Jesus how they could feed five thousand hungry men with only five barley loaves and two small fishes. From their human perspective, the only sensible solution was to send the multitude away so that they could go get their own food. You can clearly see their lack of adequate resources influencing their decision here. However, Jesus was teaching the disciples to be focused on and influenced by God's unlimited riches rather than their own lack and insufficiency.

If a broke person inherited millions of dollars from a relative, wouldn't that person have immediate resources to take care of his financial needs, especially if all his debts were also paid off? It would be unreasonable for that person to keep all his inheritance in a savings account while struggling to make ends meet for the rest of his life.

When we became one with Christ, we immediately became rich and wealthy after we inherited all the riches in glory by Christ Jesus (Eph. 1:3). Since those riches are laid up in a heavenly treasury and not in some earthly bank account, we need to understand how to translate or "convert" what we have in the spiritual realm to the natural realm. There is no currency in heaven. What is in heaven is *power* to get wealth. As 1 Corinthians 1:24 says, "Christ is the power of God, and the wisdom of God." And what we have been discussing is how the power to get material wealth and riches is revealed to you in a form of wisdom that allows you to overcome any particular lack or insufficiency.

Proverbs 3:14 says that the "proceeds of wisdom *are* better than the profits of silver, and her gain than fine gold" because wisdom gives you not only riches and honor, but also eternal life (Prov. 3:16). As you think the thoughts of Christ on wealth and riches, God reveals wisdom to you about what you need to do specifically to manifest your power for wealth in any particular situation. God's instructions for you might be totally different from what He tells another believer in a similar situation, since every situation is different. God can put a beautiful melody in your heart that will hit the billboards as the number one song and bring you riches, or He may give you a business idea, a book, a skill, an invention, etc. God has uncountable ways for you to manifest His power for wealth. You have to renew your mind with the thoughts of Christ so that you can hear specific instructions from God about any situation.

Psalms 119:130 says that the entrance of God's word gives light, and 2 Peter 1:19 says that "we have also a more sure word of prophesy; whereunto ye do well that ye take heed, as unto a light that shineth in a dark place, until the day dawn, and the day star arise in your hearts." When we consider those two scriptures together, we learn that the light from God's word does not come with just mental knowledge of that word. Rather, because we love the word of God, we spend time thinking about it until the word releases light into our heart in the form of a new revelation or inspiration to do something we would not have done before. However, every revelation or inspiration must be tested and confirmed by other scriptures. That revelation or inspiration is the wisdom we are discussing here.

It is not that what you have in your hand is not enough to satisfy your needs. It is not that the five loaves and two fishes in the little boy's hands were not enough to feed five thousand men. It is not that Peter's fishing business was struggling. It is not that your eyes are not good enough to see. It is not that your legs are not good enough to walk, or your cells good enough to fight the disease in your body. Whatever few resources you have are all God needs to manifest His solution to the problem you may be facing. In fact, God specializes in situations wherein there is *nothing* to work with except your faith in Him, so that people may believe that He is the one who calls those things that are not as though they were! So never look down on what you have in your hands, because all you need is God's wisdom on how to use what you already have.

In all of this, remember that the purpose of wealth and riches is always to advance the kingdom of God on the earth; it is never about accumulating riches on the earth for our own personal agendas.

As you seek to advance the kingdom of God (saving souls, giving to the needy, supporting the preaching of the gospel, etc.), God makes available to you everything you need to help you bear more fruit.

Beloved, I wish above all things that thou mayest prosper, and be in health even as thy soul prospereth.

(3 John 1:2)

Chapter 11

Salvation

As you already know, the purpose of Jesus Christ was to please the Father by giving his life a ransom for many. Although Jesus had a choice not to die, he submitted himself to a very painful and shameful death to save man. He knew that he was the only way to the Father, and without his sacrifice, all men would continue to be oppressed by the devil and eventually end up in hell. But aren't we grateful that Jesus did not change his mind in the garden? Jesus gave up *everything* to ensure that we could have and enjoy life to the full until it overflows! Oh, what a savior is our Lord! I just want to take a moment to say THANK YOU JESUS!

In the mind of Jesus, nothing on earth was more important than finishing the work his Father sent him to do. Not even his necessary food and drink could undermine that agenda.

The parable about the lost sheep in Luke 15 gives us more insight into the mind of Christ when it comes to saving the lost.

While he has already taken care of those who have been saved, Jesus' primary focus is on those who are yet to be saved. Following the parable of the lost sheep, Jesus told a similar story about a prodigal son. Just like any caring father, the father of the prodigal son had missed his son and wanted him back home. I believe that the reason he saw his returning son at a great distance was because he was so often looking out, far into the distance, to see if his son was coming back home!

When a parent loses his child today, he enlists the help of the police and even posts all kinds of rewards for information that would lead him to the missing child. So it wouldn't be a stretch to imagine that the father of the prodigal son would have appreciated anyone who would have helped his son come back home. As a loving Father, God is always looking out to see who finds the way back to Him. If you place God in the 'shoes' of the father of the prodigal son, you can begin to understand how much God appreciates soul winners.

Yet the senior brother of the prodigal son was out of touch with his father because he was busy with everything except the main thing on his father's heart. If he had requested some resources and a few servants to go in search of his missing brother, I'm sure his father would have given him some advice and sent him on his way. But his concern was neither with his younger brother nor with why his father was often looking out into the distance. His father's stuff was more important to him. Since he did not understand his father's agony, he also did not understand his father's excitement.

Thank God that we have a senior brother, Jesus, who left the splendor of his majesty in heaven, took on the form of a man, and came to earth just to help us back home! Unlike the brother of the prodigal son, Jesus is right there with God when God is rejoicing over one sinner who gets saved!

Jesus wants us to have the same mind-set about saving the lost. He does not want us to play the role of the uncaring senior brother; neither does he want us to play the role of the other ninety-nine "sheep" that were just waiting for the return of their shepherd. Rather, he wants us to get involved with the work: go into the world, preach the gospel, and help others to be reconciled with God.

When you think about it, you don't even have to wait until you get into full-time ministry or go to another country before you can lead someone to Christ. There are unbelievers all around us. Earlier Christians sacrificed their lives, received lashes, remained jailed in smelly dungeons, suffered shipwrecks, were crucified upside down, and basically gave up everything to ensure that everyone could get an opportunity to hear the gospel of Jesus Christ. Their work has made our work so much easier today. Statistically, based on a population of two billion Christians in the world, every Christian would have to lead only two people to Christ for the whole world to be saved! But just like the ninety-nine sheep in the story of the lost sheep, most people don't concern themselves with soul winning. One study found that less than 2 percent of Christians actually engage in soul winning[1].

If you renew your mind to conform to the mind of Christ in the area of saving the lost, you will find that God is ready to provide everything you need to lead people to Christ. Jesus said, "You know the saying, 'Four months between planting and harvest.' But I say, wake up and look around. The fields are already ripe for harvest. The harvesters are paid good wages, and the fruit they harvest is people brought to eternal life. What joy awaits both the planter and the harvester alike!" (John 4:35–36 NLT).

__Situational Soul Winning__

The Holy Spirit makes soul winning as simple and easy as recommending a good movie or restaurant to someone: with excitement, you tell him enough about the movie or restaurant to make him desire the same experience you had. The gospel of Jesus Christ is a love story that is never intended to condemn or make anyone feel sad. Rather, the message is intended to fill people's hearts with joy and hope for a better life in Christ Jesus. When you minister to someone, maybe a total stranger, a friend, or a family member, all you are doing is giving him a free gift of eternal life.

Here is the bottom line: since the unbeliever already knows that he is a sinner, all you need to explain to him is that despite his imperfections, the grace of God has qualified him to receive the free gift of salvation. He just needs to believe in his heart and confess with his mouth that Jesus is Lord and that he is the one who died and rose up again for his sins. Also explain to him that the free gift of salvation includes the right to have eternal life, healing, deliverance, freedom, peace, joy, righteousness, prosperity, and hope in the Lord!

Situational soul winning involves striking up a casual conversation with someone with the intent of ultimately telling him about the grace of God for salvation. You goal is to lead him to pray the sinner's prayer. Most of the time, people are so grateful when we spend a few minutes of our time to help them receive God's free gift of eternal life: "For whosoever shall call upon the name of the Lord shall be saved. How then shall they call on him in whom they have not believed? And how shall they believe in him of whom they have not heard? And how shall they hear without a preacher? And how shall they preach, except they be sent? As it is written, How beautiful are the feet of them that preach the gospel of peace, and bring glad tidings of good things!" (Rom. 10:13–15).

Jesus says to every believer, "Go into all the world and preach the Good News to everyone. Anyone who believes and is baptized will be saved. But anyone who refuses to believe will be condemned" (Mark 16:15–16 NLT).

The Sinner's Prayer

Dear heavenly Father, I know that I am a sinner. But today I repent and turn away from my sins. I believe in my heart and confess with my mouth that Jesus Christ is Lord. Come into my heart and save me. I ask in the name of Jesus. Amen!

Endnotes

[1] Evangelism Statistics. (2009). Retrieved June 22, 2014 from https://bible.org/illustration/evangelism-statistics

Notes

About the Author

Fred Ato Kwamina Adomako is a member of the soul winning ministry in his local church, through which he gets the privilege to minister salvation to many people in the New York City area. For more than a decade, Fred has been passionately involved with various community outreach programs designed to share the love of God and help people meet their spiritual, physical, and social needs.

Fred lives in New Jersey with his wife and children. You can contact him by e-mail at FredAdomako.TLJ@gmail.com.

www.ingramcontent.com/pod-product-compliance
Lightning Source LLC
Chambersburg PA
CBHW072105290426
44110CB00014B/1839